REGENERATION MACHINE

# Regeneration Machine

## Joe Denham

◊ NIGHTWOOD EDITIONS | 2015

Nightwood Editions
P.O. Box 1779
Gibsons, BC VON 1VO
Canada
www.nightwoodeditions.com

TYPOGRAPHY & COVER DESIGN: Carleton Wilson

Cover image created from illustrations found in *Our Seamarks;*
*a plain account of the Lighthouses,... Buoys, and Fog-signals*
*maintained on our Coasts*, courtesy of the British Library.

Nightwood Editions acknowledges financial support
from the Government of Canada through
the Canada Book Fund and the Canada Council for the Arts,
and from the Province of British Columbia through
the British Columbia Arts Council and the Book Publisher's Tax Credit.

This book has been produced on 100% post-consumer recycled,
ancient-forest-free paper, processed chlorine-free
and printed with vegetable-based dyes.

Printed and bound in Canada.

CIP data available from Library and Archives Canada.

ISBN 978-0-88971-317-8

*In Memoriam*
Nevin Sample
1973–1995

There is an ache inside that Gordian knot, the brain,
which wants to do so much in so many directions.

—Tomas Tranströmer

The block hung like the bled carcass of everything
that's carried us to what we've become. It swung
slowly on its chain as wind gusted through
the funnel of the deck awning's arc. Stripped bare
to its singular chunk of machined solid steel,
it spun like a marionette strung from a wheel.
I could feel its weight though its weight rose
through the chain to the beam, loading the hoist's
four posts. The feeling was fleeting, a ghost.

Driving home in dusk's diffuse grey dimming,
the asphalt, slick with rain, blazed golden
as late sun spilt over the trees. The aura
of the day died. Darkness seeped out
from the firs, blooming in the world beyond
my windshield as the highway swept seaside
to where I'd swerved over the soft shoulder,
orgasm flaring aurora across my mind, a rush
of dust trailing the car as it slid from the road

into the broom. That was well over a decade past.
I was young. She was younger. The taste of her
blood on my tongue didn't linger, though following
the crash, for a long thoughtless instant, I suckled
the head wound—pardon the pun—where
the console carved its corner, on impact, into her
skull. It was the small sound in her throat that I
recalled, the one she'd made, like sad laughter, saying,
*It's all fun and games, Joseph, till somebody gets hurt.*

I pulled the truck over where the broom breaks
to the shore. There was little then stopping me
from not stopping, from letting the long box
follow me into the chuck. I rolled a smoke
and thought of my as-of-late-piss-poor luck
while smoke curled about the cab. The sea
spread out like a thick slab of slate, roiling
in the wind, as the cherry burnt like light
off a wire. Let's just say there is a fire.

And each thought is an injector ionizing the fuel,
the fuel igniting in the hole. This is as close
to the soul, or a vague sketch of the shadow of
its silhouette, as I'll come. I'm uncertain
what to believe of what does and does not occur
orbiting the sun. I let the diesel rumble and thrum,
each cylinder drumming its small compressive thunder
over the counterpoint of waves pounding the beach
as I huddled to the warmth whirring from the fan

and thought of your heart as it ran and ran and
for what? So it could break like a crash test
car crumpling against the brick wall of your brain,
its self-effacement, its pain? So you sent a bullet
straight into your skull. And that was that, wasn't it,
sorry friend? Sorry world, sorry witness, sorry
wind that sang through steel railings the sound of
bearings beginning to seize, their spinning straining,
as I climbed out into the rain and walked down

to be as close as I could to the gathering storm as
it heaved and sheared off the strait. It was getting late,
night gathering too, the islands' distant lights like a static
strand of stardust on the horizon. *As close as I can come,*
*which isn't very,* I was thinking, my thinking sinking
and sinking with the weight and violence of what
you once needed, my rejection cold as my chosen
occupation, the heavy block of that B-series Cummins
hanging like the garbage guts of my trade, our trade,

the last knot that bound us before you slid your finger
over that trigger and the afternoon unwound under
the shatter of the hammer. For years I could barely
stammer my own name, and then I was there,
in the leaden late light of that storm, choosing.
I awoke alone the next morning with the sun cold-
calling through the window. There was an angel
pruning her nails, backlit, on the sill. The backspin
of a bicycle's freewheel streamed sibilant through my street-

level window, the rider's voice singing over the click and whir.
The trick is to not do a double take. The trick is one
of light and of the mind and of wanting to believe we
aren't alone, in our hideous accumulation, without
the possibility of more than what we find when we look
upon the day finally, sleep rinsed from our eyes, and see.
That morning I heard the heavenly host of my own vestigial
hope lobbing lies over the waking border. I yearned to believe.
Since then I've learned to leave such moments like a child

learns finally that lifting the fish from its pond leaves
it frightened, then frozen, then gone. Which is to say
there is a long stretch of vacant sky between what
I can imagine and what I can try. I took the day
to recuperate, recalibrate. Left the dry beast hanging
from its hook; shook loose the thick dust of winter
in the new season's first light; read some pages of
yet another dead, much-redacted book. I learned to cook.
I stood my ground against Bogdan with two pawns and a rook.

While we played there was a corvid clonk-clonking
on a wire overhead. Taunting us, it seemed, though
anthropomorphizing is like the angel: a fool's dream.
*I've seen what I've seen*, Bogdan insisted, telling
a story of a sister speaking in tongues and a light
so bright it was like staring at the noonday sun.
*What do you make of that?* Not much. I'd given up
by then trying to believe, disbelieve or understand,
as such, content as I was to listen to the lilt of

his Slavic speech; to reach that place where it's enough,
much more than enough, to be alive in the alternately
writhing and thriving world, in good company,
airing out like long-used linens finally shook
and hung on the line. There, in a moment in time.
Then the sunshine sputtered out, eclipsed by a dark
cumulus from the southeast. The air we were airing in
altered, charged and cold, and the afternoon began
to fold (like a Murphy bed, like the thoughts in my head)

swiftly into night. My wife once knew a man who'd fallen
three times from the sky in his hot air balloon. He remained,
she says, an enthusiast into his later years despite
the consecutive crashings of his basket to the ground.
He was one of those rare dogs Seligman found who
learned resilience instead of helplessness though the
random flarings of intense pain he (Seligman) delivered
through a wire undoubtedly seemed inexplicable and
uncontrollable (to the dogs) as fire. It's how the music

resonates from the lattice bracing and spruce though
it's been fifteen years since focal dystonia morphed
Bruce's picking fingers into one dumb thumb. He sits
as though in prayer before the liquor store, over his
beloved guitar, and plays slow so his mind has time
to sort out the signals, and the notes come clean
and gleam, a Rilkean dream of sweet tone drifting
over the din of idling cars and idle chatter. What
matters is the bone and breath of being. Really. I was

seeing as through a veil of mist as the rain and cold
clenched the coastline in its fist. It was nothing explicable,
that hazed sight, as we broke from our stalemate
and gathered our wrappings, our glasses, the board
and its pieces, as it is nothing I can explain here still.
It is a weakness in the design or the construction
of the will. I go about at times with an unstable
list, heeled too far to starboard or port, put so by
something within me or without, I can't say (perhaps

both are one and the same, I'll come to understand
at the end of the day). At the end of *that* day
I drove down the long hill to the docks, the wind
again (that year it seemed perpetually) snapping
the flags taut from their poles, raising a symphony
of chimes and rustlings over the bay. I'd meant only
to check on the engine suspended from its hoist,
survey the dock lines and alarms, bilge pumps and
voltmeters. But then it was a presence like the antithesis

of that which had preened on my sill in the waking
dawn: an absence of light lifting off the water;
an arrangement of shadows and the old child-sight
that spikes the adrenals with fear. It was clear
I needed to lie down. So I crawled into the fo'c'sle
and let the darkness do what darkness does:
allows us to abscond, fallows our wordly bond.
It follows, doesn't it, that we learn to love it so,
the further we go, the further we give ourselves

over to the capital-d Darkness of Being; Of Being
Adult; Of Being Adult In the New and In EveryWhichWay
Sweetfucked Millennium? But in sleep it's swept clear:
the fear, the anxiety, the interplay of shame and intention
and failure we endure—or if not swept, distilled,
discomfited. Pitted of its essential substance.
So, its stranglehold loosened: my mind then a vessel
within a vessel within a vessel, lulled in the loving
languishing of the sea sloshing against the hull-

planks like lugubrious laughter. Like liquid fire
warming the cold core carried within since before
Prometheus lost his eyes to Kratos once he'd
thieved the flame, which is to say, there was desire
before there was fire, or at least that's what I was
thinking upon waking (this time unvisited),
though I could have been and likely am wrong,
it's kind of chicken vs. egg, and I suspect it will be
till the final leg of this journey is good and done:

daylight and its horrible insistence again, an earnest
uncle ready to school you in the ways of the world
of work, *First light sonny boy you can sleep when you're dead!*
Some mornings I can feel the whole thing caving,
our entire sorry stupid structure built of rationale and style,
dishonesty and hope and fear, I can feel it buckle and wince,
like a flooded bulkhead near bursting. Do I need
something clever here to smooth this over? A swilled-pint
parable or pun, perhaps a mention of personal fallibility

or something with that scripted, despite-it-all shimmer?
The morning I was born a young woman put her lips
(full and red) to mine (tiny, blue) and for that first
precarious hour forced into me the precious air
my premature, half-formed lungs couldn't draw.
The ambulance's flashing lights tore open the darkness
like a skip-toothed saw. From an overpassing plane
it must have seemed something like a flashing, lone
and low-crawling insect. Inside the hurtling aluminum

and steel she steadied, bracing herself against the lean
of corners, and breathed. Oxygen. Blood. Momentum.
I awoke in that fo'c'sle, parched and disoriented
in the base-oil blackness and bilge stench, wanting only
to dissolve like salt into water. I had that pre-migraine
feeling like the liquid composition of my body was
a tailings pond, toxic sludge, while the rain fell like
a chorus of gladness on the deck above me. Can I
come flat out and say here I can't carry the discrepancy

between the discomfort and beauty with dignity?
I can't. I move tentatively, bewildered, through
this miasmic array: the colours, the contours, the clear span
between perception's and inception's sway. What
was it I sang with such conviction yesterday? I'd
like to build an ark, I thought, high on the precipice
above the gravel pit above town, and spurn the hecklers
with the furrow of my sweated brow as I bolt yellow cedar
over steam-bent fir. It's sculpture. It's how I feel about

smart meters cell phones wi-fi sprayed crops cellophane
and this whole mess of privileging economy over humanity.
My ark. My pious act of protest in my lonely imagination
that morning as I languished in the single shaft of diffuse
daylight and downdrifting dust that worked its way
from aft of the cabin down the companionway to my bunk
before I rose finally from dreaming below the waterline
and sobered belatedly to what I'd become, and also to knowing
you were gone. Sometimes the mistakes of the past aren't made

right or easier to bear with time, but more apparent and shameful:
regret, like a misdiagnosis that nevertheless defines us. Or the missed
diagnosis my father lived with for decades before non-virulent
lymphoma disintegrated his spleen. I'd like to go back there,
to that fo'c'sle and that final dream, and remember. These days
it seems impossible to believe that anything was so unclear
as the years I lived before that morning: withering, wandering
always with a sense of somehow being stranded beyond life
as though my body were a weir between myself and my

rightful world, an ungraspable elsewhere I cowered from
whenever a vision would overcome me before dusk or dawn
as I swept the town's sidewalks clean in the pale mists
of the winters, sodden and cold, of my early adolescence;
and later, staring down groundlines winding up from the depths
I could only imagine (igneous-cragged, glass-sponged, aphotic)
each in-season night as I'd try to steady my mind for a few precious
hours of sleep before rising to the wind and dark whirling about the deck
the way it did around the stripped block I began with here. Yesterday

I gave a lecture on work and water and art in a room built entirely of concrete
without a single window through which light might enter. Somehow the soul
doesn't understand the tyranny of corners. I can speak for hours and hours and
afterwards, in the night, not know the difference between love and hate
and which worked my tongue, with what force and intent, from which source
and why. Once, in one vestigial grove of Garry oaks, I swept the air
about my body till it was clear as the trees' auras exhaling into the grasses
and bees and all the blooming bursting beyond sidewalks and dust. These days
there's money, that anxiety, the endless barrage of what need be done

and the children wanting only, ultimately, attention and kindness.
There are people inhabiting the streets of the cities because
it's always so hard to keep from hanging your head in your hands,
from becoming something or someone you always knew you
never would. Sharp and unkind, wingless. Wonderless. August
asks me from his car seat, in the midst of a slow seaside drive,
rain pattering the window he's been gazing from, *So, does
the universe just go on forever then, or what?* And I'm thinking
first of what a mind he must have, and from where?—before

the sad thought settles in, the selfish thought, of his future
loss of innocence, of this wonderment he's beaming with
diminishing with knowledge, which is ultimately only myself
mourning my own losses, isn't it? So I answer, *Yes, forever, son,*
*it just keeps on going, on and on, isn't that something?*
What are we doing trying to make sense of things
from the enclosure of rooms without windows, within walls
built of poison dust? Some of my first memories are
of my father and uncle and grandfather belted, tooled, raising

walls and a roof somewhere in the heat of my fifth or sixth summer.
Standing back on a pile of sawdust studying what it seemed to mean
to be a man. The strain and anger and ease. Now, with my uncle long
passed into his self-asphyxiation, and the cancer in my father's blood
weakening him to a life of prayer and inertia, I lay out the centres,
fasten the rafters, deck the ceiling to keep out the rain, wind, moon
and stars—while my son watches with wonder below. Perhaps
growing is an evolving sense of grasping that there is nothing
and nobody to follow. Ice on the subfloor at dawn. Ice crumbling

underfoot below blue breaking through black over the near eastern slope.
This is the eternal stillness. The one that will always unsound like
the last of a bell's chiming ringing below any range of hearing
in the endless days and hours long after we've left. Nothing
and nobody, and nowhere to follow to. For now, still, we break
the stillness open. Machine-dig the footings deep below
the frost line and send the blast of each nail shot or struck ricocheting
through the forest over the roaring highway across the valley. Take the air
into our lungs and exhale our banter and complaint, the rising

cost of living and the cold in our bones and the deceit
our complaint complies with when not only the poor overseas
and the poor on East Hastings suffer, but so too the whales
and sharks and sea turtles, the corals dying off in scorched southern seas.
Still, we are on our knees, and knees weaken. Which breeds a fear
akin to the fear I felt in the dark of that fo'c'sle at dawn like rain
feeds rot right to the heart of a windfall tree wherein insects
nest and swarm, and thrive in the warming world, blackening
countries of forest, the pines overrun valley after valley, the firs

and hemlocks too, while feller bunchers process the stands
for hog fuel and pallet lumber, fodder for the growth of emerging
markets. The last time I saw you, when you turned from me,
I could sense your future like a black hole opening as your back
receded from view. I stood in the doorway and watched, but
there was nothing I could do just as there is nothing I can do
beyond this daily rising and working and breathing and trying
somehow to find the necessary balance to keep my cynicism
from being the legislator of my days, to keep compassion

and kindness as alive as your eyes were when you looked
out over the water, from the deck of your dilapidated boat,
and thought for the first time how beautiful the world
would remain in the close and coming days without you.
I know you felt the sadness of the sea bind in your bones
as you set your traps alone into the dark, currented depths.
This summer we hauled through bloom so thick each trap
left a swirling black tunnel on the surface as it burst through
on the line. This could mean the beginning of the end

of life. These days, some days, it seems anything and
everything could or does signify the same. There should be
no shame in saying so, though it's a constant struggle
to keep the truth of the trajectory in sight when the night
wants only to lay us down, in the easy light of flashing
screens and the soft down of polished sitcoms, to feel nothing
if not forgiven. Pleased and appeased. Off the hook
like a fish finally free of the fought line. I'm remembering
a time when I harangued my mother each day for just another

hour of television oblivion, then passed the nights staring into
a bright bedside bulb so the dark wouldn't pull me away
into the elsewhere I knew was right there, surrounding me
like a windstorm unseen. Now my son struggles through
the same night fears and need and I find empathy only
under the odd small rock inside me, occasionally, and ponder
at the end of each workday, that desert: desperation: the dirt
and the heat and the light. It's too often that doing and feeling
what's right seems nothing but a fool's errand along

a bitter road. But then there are days. Days!
Days when the energy arrives and gladness explodes
somewhere deep down (beneath the manic mind; the
slow burning soul) so it permeates everything inscaped
and all intention with compassion and kindness and love.
It's the dichotomy of dwelling inside such a dark cave
with a glorious fire burning always at its centre that sets
everything up as question without answer, thirst
without water. We were walking the highway together

late in our youth, the pitch dark cloaking us, no stars,
weed in our blood, the ditches running, cheap booze
on the brain, T-shirts, late fall, first frost chill on
the thick forest air, high firs and cedars and stillness
by the roadside, our breathing rhythmic and a hint of
fear between us, no streetlights, no headlights on-
coming, no moon, the gun tucked like a promise
in your pocket, an incubating sickness, pressure
accumulating just as it does along the fault line

we'd spent our lives upon always with that sense
of the ground about to give out or crumble or heave
beneath our feet. No wonder, then, the nihilism.
And now the awareness of a world overrun to ruin
by bad governance and negligent citizenry, no wonder
the nihilism, safety in the hollow note and careful hues
of grey, the frightened philosopher's endless heartache
blues, the last-light hotel and midnight bar swan song
sung solo by everyone, in unison. I was at the helm

of a fifty-five foot Wahl-built troller bucking tide down
Johnstone Strait in the wee hours, end of the season,
night-still, approaching the narrows, low sad lowing of a distant
or near foghorn across the channel, the sodium bulb blazing into
a veil of swirling grey, red-eyed in the green radar light,
coffee and diesel, cold hands and workboat filth, dark water
tipping the hull in the tide-churn, the Jimmy rumbling,
reliable: at eight knots everything suspended as we navigated
Ripple Rock and I thought to think of that one morning in the base-oil

black fo'c'sle when I realized then and there that a hybrid of self-
pity and pragmatic realism was definitely the answer. Oh, I was always
that kid with his arm reaching to high heaven the teacher ignored, cursing
my know-it-all confidence and aplomb. Fuck it. This world done me wrong!
And you too, no doubt, have your bones, no? So why not stoop,
sink low, slum it up together in the late or early glow of this,
our despicable opulence? I like mine crass and straightforward, a hint of
regret and sincerity in the aftertaste—the head's heady counterpoint
to feet stained by years of barefoot walking between rows of seeds

planted and pollinated beneath high westerly winds. At times I watch
from a distance as Amy wipes her brow and digs her seedlings in.
There's only hope in the simplest things now, the rings of brown and green
inside the irises of her eyes I have mistaken for god and iron bars
and portals to her soul which might still know me long after and before
we both leave and arrive here. Her small spade turns the earth and the Earth
turns so quickly we can't comprehend, ask anyone old, time's a whisper
and a song and we're gone. I see the last surge of youth in her shoulders,
the stray greys in her dark hair falling to the ground, her breasts and

thighs and knees and ankles and toes falling too, lined fingers
full of music falling, tiny hands growing tired, taking root:
how will I live if I'm the last to go? And as selfish as the sentiment is
I ask it as a prayer, the only prayer I can utter as I feel the turn
in me to errancy vis-a-vis some latent Christianity I've yet
to eradicate from the place in me that probably wants Mommy
always to approve my spirituality. There's something Oedipal here,
primal, or perhaps it's just that beside me as I write the dog is
humping the couch. Good pooch! Another notch on the old

bedpost, so to speak, which is just another dose of weak medicine
for the fear of abandoning irony for the lofts of sincerity, high
and lonely. How 'bout we get high on shwag and watch Penn play
Spicoli instead? Or rework the Dark Lady sonnets in the voice of
Snuffleupagus to Bird? I know you, like I, have thought recently
of the essential chaos and the limits of our comprehensions and/
or constructions of beauty, so why not smoke a fatty and listen
to "Visions of Johanna" from the digitally remastered, reissued
boxset *Biography*? It's just like the night to bring out the irreverent

and mindful—ain't it?—like we're tiptoeing blindfolded backwards
towards the sacred. Stumbling with every step. Too heavy a load
of useless cargo, the entire continent drowning in plastic corporate
junk, the children with Christmas and heartburn and I don't know
how to turn my eyes or theirs away though the sea is suffocating
and so little of how we live is sensible, even sane. So we build
a house, a garden, a man, a woman, four corners and a fenceline
as though our settling might somehow suspend time while the kids
simultaneously grow and learn to know, by some miracle, better.

And that's what you're missing, old friend. It's that simple.
Sure, we're deluded and distasteful in our hubris and entitlement,
but the love of a good woman, and children, and a home
raised with one's own hands. I can tell you beauty is a constant,
like pi, and light; we don't create it the way no god
created us and the creatures of the ocean we've killed.
You were searching for something in Leviticus when you left us.
Some anecdote for chaos. But you must have known the book
was not our book and the bullet you loaded finally into

that chamber was meant for no life but your own. Stone
within stone. We're not born alone—bathed as we are
in our mother's strain to survive—but we can live and die so.
And do. Adrift as we are inside this endless blue, the same sky
stretching over those other winds of childhood and the storm
that, unceasing, unsettles us inside ourselves even now, and always,
even with the dead as close as a whisper, a lover—I know
I can't comprehend it, there are no corners, no cardinal points:
when I strike my voice out into the air, cleaving, it is a clearing

in late summer, late light, there is muscle in the waves, spirit,
insects swarming the grasses, filaments in the bending and unbending
brightness: you are alone waiting for your guests to arrive,
the hour is set and then this unplanned reprieve, you feel the ghosts
like the inner skin of a balloon blown around you, there must be
a magnet at the centre of the soul, or there is no soul, or the Earth
makes its medicine and everything you've learned leads to madness,
lends the light an opacity and the gathering dark its counterpoint, clarity.
But how then do we reconcile the dwindling elegance with the absurdity of

Elon Musk's wish to die on Mars? Oh, outmoded me! I'm living
through our way of life, a fishery, an industry, disintegrating
in the acid of colonial guilt, my tongue lashed down like the wrists
of the unrepentant thief on Calvary. There's a photo of my great-great-
grandmother on my study wall, her Cree neck framed tight in
white Victorian collar lace, but it's always and only heard
in the context of race when I say there are no sacred lands
or they all are; to claim a piece of earth as conquered or unceded
is to hold the world like a child might a caught fish as it suffocates

out of water. It is fire with fire fought, every assumption of
entitlement aching in the bones of the biosphere. I like the cinematique
chorography of my daughter midwinter in the lazy river
at the local rec centre, her athletic dolphinesque swimming through
the chlorinated water and her unimpeded joy, floating and begoggled,
grace and fluidity, a reminiscence of our piscine origin. Yet let us
not diverge: you drove a bullet into your brain: the rain still
thrums on the roof of this house I built board by board, square,
level, plumb, while I write to you red-eyed, insomniatic, each precious

breath of my children and wife counting the night down though
you'll never know them and these words will burn like a candle
in the noonday sun. *Yo ho ho and a bottle of rum,* we'd sing, strung
out between shifts at sea and benders and hope, that sickest of opiates
(Marx missed the mark there, wouldn't you say, comrade? Eh?)
and then we'd take another run at the walls, the whiskey, the distance
between us in this cold northern country just a way of surviving,
though you let that wind strip you down to bare flesh and sorrow:
this is my last draft, requiem, I won't stand forth and sing

for forgiveness beyond this: there was a moment when you turned
away and I dropped anchor and did not follow. Whatever it will allow
I ask of it now. I dream of music and wake to my iPhone vibing
on the windowsill. Amy breathes so silently when she sleeps
sometimes I have to reach out just to be sure she's still here, and
our children in their room beyond the wall: the fear makes me
insular, insouciant to other's suffering: it's anathema: without
a god there are only these hands, these tiny hearts, this struggle
to strive for extraordinary capacity amidst the day-to-day

stresses and sicknesses, the precipice of time unwinding.
First there's dreaming of what you'll become, then there's
wondering what you could have been, then finally there's
less and less reason not to have a few pints after work; less
music burning a hole in what may or may not be the soul.
We were nearly two hundred miles offshore when the blood
started heaving up from my gut this past summer, there was
no stopping the rhythmic convulsions, the tunas' blood and mine
bile-laced, intermingling on the old fir decking, the sea

in it too, everywhere, the endless blue and high westerly waves
towering over us hour upon hour unceasing, no stopping
any of it, no way out, the tuna schooling northward, compressor
pounding, night hauling the frantic creatures astern, walleyed,
rigid, the staccato slap of their death throes on the gutting board,
my body and theirs convulsing, more blood, the hollow light
of the sodiums casting it all in sepia, burning dull and fierce
under a firmament of stars more numerous than imaginable.
The weakness I knew then in that churning gut of storm

I carry with me now, a dark seed of knowledge that helps me
understand why you brought that barrel to your temple
and pulled the trigger. Remember with me what it means
to stand blood-drenched in the wailing wind over a heap
of silvered bodies bleeding out before you, remember
the knife holds you, the billions of our species needing
this flesh and this nurturing, the sea's spirit coursing in
the schools and swarms, migration, momentum, the cold
and warm currents colliding, we're coming closer and

closer to the beginning, the sea is convulsing while
congress makes another circus of sequestration and
the consumer confidence index comes in lower
than anticipated, though the VIX shrugs it off, the Dow
surging up on pre-earnings optimism. I made contrarian
bullish plays on SPWR, TSLA and GLW, sat on my hands
while the consolidations solidified, then felt the rush
of self-satisfaction when each in turn achieved the coveted
Golden Cross, rising above their fifty- and two-hundred-day SMAS

and rallying up into the stratosphere of market cap heaven.
Every man in the Hale family has taken his own life
in his later years for as long as anyone can remember. Late
September, Arden, Ontario, passing through on tour,
Isaac and I shoot a game of pool on the table I was
to be born on before the labour became prolonged,
then sit out on his stoop and sip hooch in the early evening
din of cicadas while he tells me he's decided to end the curse
with himself. It's not that I don't know what to say (clearly!) in these

situations, it's the weight of words and ideas that won't
be buoyed no matter how well built the vessel—it's only
the brain, we know so little—Isaac speaks as though
preoccupied with some elsewhere: the gravel road
that scuffed his knees over and over, the long grass fields
where he learned to look inward in the evening light. It's love
that sits down between us as the lone and dim streetlight
sputters on. There's too much history. He wants
chickens and a goat but the new bylaws disallow it

and the bureaucrats he's fighting wouldn't know Weber
from the hole in the ground left after digging up Max's
petrified femur, which Isaac and I'd both like to use
to club them silly so they might slow down, drink
some hooch, and stop overcrowding the world with
policy. Too much history. In a perfect economy
we'd all dance naked at the Beltane fires and bed
the virgin fawn before daybreak. Then Starbucks,
Pilates, a verse or two of *The Diamond Cutter*

and focus: another day to dominate and conquer!
Amy and I spent years out on Lasqueti allowing
the silence dominion, the long evening walks
past Bergens' farm, the unkempt graveyard shrouded
in shadow, millennial firs and maples gnarled
and forked like frozen fire. All good healing
occurs in quiet sunshine and night's natural darkness.
We spoke little of what it was we were doing there:
a pair of hands fumbling blindly for something

to hold fast to. To be married is to learn to trust and leave
everything necessary and substantial unuttered: my love,
the lines that haunt your hands and face, the other worlds
your spirit inhabits, hold fast to me, I won't waver. We're
nowhere, together, trying to collect enough courage to
meet the day, each day, the children hungry for everything
in the world sad and joyous, the cold cold currents colliding
with the warm, everything running, no changing any of it, there's
a flock of ghosts perched on my carved-out Helicon chest

and I can't rise up from this long and fitful sleep. We're drowning
in liquidity and the Fed's still printing money. So many say it's the end
of retirement and cheap pomegranates, and they say so as though
sadness were appropriate here: shortly after the initiation of
further quantitative easing, Fukishima's melting cores breached
containment; there's cesium-137 in the rain and therefore the
lettuce, milk, fish; I don't know what I'll say when they ask us
two decades from now why we didn't at least pull stakes and run
from the fallout; officially, core inflation is stable and there is

no significant threat to human health, methodologies and standards
having been adjusted accordingly: we've moved far beyond
speculation and conspiracy into the anemic marrow of
bureaucracy and I can't remember the last time I read a tidy
little metaphor without feeling nostalgia and disgust. Art's
inadequacy is the rust on the machinery, the slipping gears of
grace and imagination: postcards from our extended five-star
vacation, poolside happy hour, daily, to eternity. Would that I
could understand Lao Tzu, I mean fully comprehend that we are

mostly water, and immalleable, so when the full moon rises over
the scrub alders and solitary fir, and the frogs strike up down
in the swamp bottom, I'll feel like singing too, or listening
with an ear to the contrapuntal current waves deep in the cove
and the pulsing liminal pull of wind in the silk thin cloud cover,
a weighty unbalancing in the wetlands, something unseasonal,
something unaccounted for, a measure of damned if we do/
damned if we don't thrown off-kilter, just so, so everything's a touch
unsettled and unsettling despite all the so-called wisdom of ages

and the benevolence of sages and frogs. *That's* social justice!
It's hope... without the e! It's the key to the great inner truth
that'll set your soul free and earn me a weekly early primetime
on the O Network, resplendent with props from Queen O(MG!)
herself. Because wealth: it's a state of mind, of being, war
and other assorted pestilences notwithstanding, the crux is to hone
and focus one's desires and follow, follow, follow, follow, follow
the yellow brick road all the way to wherever: water your beanstalk
and climb it to the Kingdom on High, or drink the apothecary's poison

and kiss your ass goodbye. I went to see a shrink the winter after
you died. Most of what I remember from that time is a wind
so wide I could walk out on the spit off Mission Point, lean
my full weight in, face-first, and weep like I was in the world's engine
room, all cylinders pounding, my mind winding and winding and
binding on the anger. Little knots, and weather. We never get over
certain motifs, certainly, and the shrink, she took my money and tried
some Gestalt and backwoods Jungian analysis before humming
some platitudes about sundogs and spring as I left for sea. What is it

inside me that wants to reach back with these arms and
unharm our errant hearts? There's enough counting of
blessings and curses here and now, the bright shot
of moonlight through the alders and firs and the first
rows of lettuce and kale bolting to seed. Some fine
evenings it's easy to see how the whole Earth is beloved.
Despite our inherent and inherited darkness, despite
the news of the world, the myriad injustices, the night
hums with that cool sheen, silvery calm, everything

healing. There is a deer being slaughtered in the forest
just beyond our home; I'm dreaming of my daughter
drowning as it screams: the coyotes yelping around,
surrounding their kill somewhere there in the dark
ravine; it carries on, crying out the panic of its blood-
draining and defeat, the sun falls dry and hot as fire
through the window, the wailing, this must have been
your mind's last sound, you were frightened, alone:
I can't decipher whether it's you or me or the deer

or my daughter who needs the hand of some god, some
sorrow that is the wellspring of a certain form, forgiveness,
to hold fast to. Suicide has no shape. It is confusion like off-
shore fog, a dream and a desperate scream interwoven,
there are no antecedents, the moment appears and
everything is foreordained as the force of gravity upon
this sweet, sullied Earth. If I could share with you the memory
of the blackness of my son's eyes, onyx, aphotic, just moments
following his birth, my joy and surprise, that it could be

so despairing, expansive, then I could give you one good reason
to unarm. You'd have lived to be somebody's father; lover; long-
lost: whatever. And I'd have lived without the cold, cold shadow
your violence set over these stunted decades. In silence
I lie supine, imagining what the moments before impact
must have felt like as Simon fell to the ungiving
ground. It's said now that the brain is malleable, elastic,
and that someday Si might walk and dance and fuck like
the man he occasionally dreams he still is when the pain sub-

sides enough to allow him sleep. There is no moral
to the story. I've grown past caring about the latest war in
Whereveristan, or wanting to understand about the Higgs
boson or the whales. I sing when I'm not on the water
killing, when the grip that burden gets on my thorax
relaxes. I sing because even my ragged and pitchy off-
key song rings true, and I can sit out on the stoop as
the day exhales into night and cast myself out with
each note off my old guitar, and the world, it sings

back to me. Survival for some of us is a balance of knowing
how and when to sing and to listen, to allow silence as
well as song, in equal measure, for as long and unwavering
as the soul (which is beyond us, composing) will. That morning,
waking below the waterline in the womb of that old hull, haunted,
I made a choice to comprehend everything here as the music of
infinite voices in dissonant harmony, singing. It's said there is
one at the centre of all things, and though that may be so
I'd like to lift Simon back onto that scaffolding and settle

his work-and-worry tired nerves so that his footing might fall
true, and the two-by-ten hold steady beneath him, that one scorching
summer afternoon his grace caved like his skull as it cratered
against concrete. We get one go-around here, there is no walking
backwards through time: regret is an eddy in the mind created
by a point in a lifetime that rages like highwater, forever altering
currents and course. Of course, that's just one of many ways
to reconcile circumstance, call it fate: we all know an entire
flock of Monarchs was early or late as it lifted off a eucalyptus

in Mendocino County that morning, all subsequent events thus
shifting the centre of Si's balance off ever-so, and merrily we go
trying earnestly to make the futility and tragedy matter. If I know
one thing it's that all winds blow without regard: we're a scatter
of leaves on air: we're nowhere, and everywhere, and the only way
I know is to surrender: take me, great stranger, whether I exceed
or falter, with time enough to know myself beloved upon this Earth.
It's not my life, but my worth, which I've measured out with coffee
spoons: how many moons will pull the water low below the littoral

mud before I relinquish my love for beer and whiskey, or the fear
that I'll amount to nothing but bones in a pile at the bottom
of the sea, cast back after death to the one thing I've known will
always receive me? It's easy to see the darkness as a lack of
light and grace, but it's a cool, clearing embrace too: I hear
Amy bathing in the next room, humming, as the walls of our home
pour time from the pores of cells so small they're unseen but
in a daydream, mind wandering. My eyes stay unfocused
on the light, intently, whenever awareness awakens inwardly

and comprehension comes full circle: there's cause for apprehension,
always, because there's gun powder in the pressure cooker and
contamination and disease, and somebody simply texting could
easily swerve into my only son on the busy highway outside of
town and sanity, it's that easy. I was standing in the kitchen doorway
when Janine told me you'd died, I was in riding shorts, helmet,
gloves and jersey, sweat stinging my eyes, one weak lamp lighting
the filthy floor dimly, you'd been there the night before, her voice
was like brittle stone, I let the phone fall to its cradle on the wall

and stood there suspended as my sweat cooled and it all settled
like a landslide into a lake. And that's what the endless cosmos
makes of us: particles of dust spilling into a fo'c'sle porthole
and I'm lost to the relevance of identity politics and who's given
their fair due or fried in the fire while we're all sucking back
the last of this world's nectar, each of us, together. Which leaves
me not pining for a world pliant as water (nor as enthralled
with Armageddon as Kevin Costner) but there's a moment
we're missing because generations of semantics stunt our tongues

trying to speak and name each nanosecond it exists. There was a time,
of course, snowfall in January, sepia-shadow, softness strung out
along barbed wire fencelines, sublime stillness in the streetlight glow,
low, low light, we'd follow our own footmarks for hours through
the rows of Cold War–era houses, a bottle of bourbon and
weed and sweetness in the limberness of body and believing
in a power and beauty people nearly never possess. We lived
with entire taxonomies of absurdity while the oil wells burned
somewhere in the Kuwaiti desert and within the red border

of a *Time* magazine cover. And us with purple hair! Piercings!
The town's *prissy faggots*, skirting the border between
Band land and the industrial park where the dark grew
like vines in our veins, the drugs the lowest hanging fruit
this working-class shithole held forth. My friend, for what it's
worth, my world's so much less without you. It's easy to feel
bitter, and I do, but there's a point where we all take the bit
and learn to choke, and spit, and let it lead us through. Though
for now I'm intent on taking one last pot shot at your past

imperfection: selfish prick, who lets his mind go so blotto
he takes a gun into a bank then runs like Franka Potente
into the forest of his own panicked ruin, pietà? See, every
last one of us is the grieving Mother Mary. Every last one
the centre and sum of the known and unknown universe
we've become. A coherent cosmology. The physical
embodiment of UDFJ-39546284 to Kingdom Come. Once was
I couldn't get past the perplex of what and where constitutes
*beyond,* by which I mean the grave and infinity and god. Now

I strip down to my pinstriped boxers and dive face-first
into the cold Salish Sea, let the green deep remind me
that right here the world is, right now the senses are,
as the skin of the arbutus is curling back, drying black,
the season stuttering on, unsettled, the garden gone
to seed as this northern land leans back into winter's
anteroom, apprehension. I've tried for comprehension
of Planck length, relativity, the quantum composition
of everything taut with the tension of a wound string

strung from bridge to nut, bowed by what beautiful, un-
benevolent hand? It's another way to understand
akin to a white bearded elderly man in the billowing
cumuli, or an underworld witch with a wand of power
and eyes of opalescent water! As it is I'm hardly fit
to ponder the absurdity of the Mexican dogs that bark
dusk till dawn out my expat hotel window. It's the sound
of the world growing hotter, of the little that's audible
to the blunt human ear. What was it you wanted, a love

lobotomized of everything left hemisphere? You must have
taken Ginsberg too seriously. You must have believed
there was something to be achieved so earnestly
it made a concave hollow in your mind when the auger
of your own mediocrity bore in. Welcome to the twenty-first century,
grotesque ghost. Join the party! Yesterday I watched a man
with no hands lick a stranger's spilt soup off the street. How's
that for exceptional? And me in my brand-new boots and
the last dying remnants of First World entitlement leaking

from my mind like urine down my leg. I'm going out
into the crooked cobble streets to howl too. It can't be
possible to sleep these days the way the brain's meant to,
deep and cool, like a river in a desert, or an elephant's
pool in the Jungle of Nool! I'm going out of my fucking
mind trying to find a way forward through this world
as it burns round and round from the inside down
to the last lame hope I can hold out and on to. I've tried
the simple repudiation of knowledge by wonder. But

we're growing sunflowers high over the asphalt driveway:
carrot, zucchini, squash and kale. We're growing darker.
The masters all knew something about perfection being
perfectly designed to fail. I find myself wondering
if kids these days feel less or more defeated by degrees
because their rejection slips arrive faster via email. I find myself
wandering a lot less at dusk, waiting instead for the slow
Ethernet connection to stream whatever mindless sitcom
I'm squandering my only life watching. I want to go back

to landlines and Cold War problems, twelve channels and
the card catalogue search. To wander the stacks, believing
in something as simple as my own precious mind, and time,
of which we all had so much, and no matter, the answers
were all there, alphabetized, cared for, and everyone went
quietly through the rooms because that was the common
courtesy, which meant something the way not heckling
at the symphony still does. Back to Dylan not advertising
cars, but singing "Dignity" with Rockin' Dopsie before

James Damiano filed suit and the Danube outflow eutrophicated
forty thousand square kilometres of the Black Sea. Which they say is
now rejuvenating just as they say the corals everywhere are dying.
This minute there are men mining salt over one thousand feet below the
bankrupt city of Detriot. I used to seek out truth like Dante's
Virgil seeking the path to the empyrean. Of course, without
the fourteenth-century flair (and probably cleaner underwear!) and
with the naïveté of a man who hadn't yet been broken on the wheel.
There's no private hell. It's the same fire that turns us all

inward, that forged your machine-crafted bullet and David
Foster Wallace's black belt: our hearts melt, or harden. Either
way, there's nothing left to pray to, and nothing left to do
but pray. So I go about my days, sadness through and through,
with a smile and a sigh and my eyes on these stilted vistas of
inner sky I whitewash with memory, withering. When the
dimming comes, what attends us, and what then of our sense
of conviction or centredness or certainty: dust and shadows and
such, I suppose, so why not live a lie so long you could walk

to the moon and back on the bridge of your nose? I lay down
a long time on that filthy lino floor listening to the fridge shutter
off and on, the landlords' Korean leaking through the ducting,
my breathing. It was something foreign. That's when I under-
stood our human weakness and the loneliness which we come
to call home. That's when I shot my love down my liver
meridian, shrunk it to pre-cancer in the organ, and left it to
cocoon and re-bloom into anger. Tonight I wake to the voices
of angels singing a song like wind: I want to begin something

without ending, finally, to find peace in the place I'm in. But
it's cold at home in this northern country and I'm leaving
again for sea, the boat's rust-rotten steel waiting
to take me farther north into darker waters yet, further
into a future set by the past that defines me: if I had
understood the claws of trajectory, the flaw of thinking
life was a clear pair of eyes, ever-opening. There's one lone
tree wavering in the forest to the east, standing against
the sky in its own swirl of wind. Which I suppose is where

Jesus came to understand we're all fallible. And all to be
forgiven. For some, that's *the* definition of freedom. It's been
almost twenty years, Nevin, since yours was the ceasing
of your own and only mind. The world's still brutal, unkind,
beautiful. Last season, a flat calm, late evening crossing
from the easy waters of Loredo Inlet to the torrid tide rip
of Cape St. James, Hecate Strait lying northwestward beneath
the sun inflating into night, burning brighter and brighter
as it breaks the horizon, the bronze over blue undulating

and I swear there's god in the waves of light and water
that surround us, a prison of perfection, it's in the dis-
placement of ocean for air, the sense of precarious
suspension, the hull plying the surface and holding us
here between low fathoms and the unfathomable heavens.
Here, for as long as luck and grace and love will allow.
I've tried and tried to convey that tension, urgency
to those who never go to sea, but each mind is wired and
mired in its own in-gazing now, and we're tired of our

selves and our everything: exhaustion: the ally and
the enemy, capitulating. One more thing: I tossed the hook
out at the head of the Cumshewa under a gallery of stars,
distant spirits, light: the language of what little I can recover
from the wreckage of an untenable wanting for god. Within
the perfect silence following, after I shut down the main engine
and the wind lay still, I slept. And those spirits, dim angels,
descended with their sorrowed hands, little shovels, huge
heart of the land and sea, ancestors, history, it all reached into

my sacrum, kidneys, and took the anger, tension, disease, anxiety,
asking simply what it was I could live without. *What is it
that you truly need, here, between the sea and the stars?* There was
smallpox on these shores, the sea otter slaughtered to near-extinction,
those wars. I lay claim to this Earth. Every height and depth, crevasse
and cove, of course it's always been mine for the taking. And yours.
We're all but inseparable from our machines now: memory-form:
manipulated amnesia. When I woke, I knew the answer. It was
elemental, dust and bone, as simple as your spread ashes sifting

down with rain into the forest dirt beside the stump you finally
sheltered behind, chest heaving, the pursuing officers taking
position across the cut, calling out. Was it clarity, then,
that final decision? The relief of just one last failure, and never
the reliving, responsibility. Twenty years Nev, and not a day
I don't wish I'd taken you in that last night, set aside
my studies, shallow ambitions, the exasperation you found
at every door: fuck your sadness, your I'm-so-lost flailing, blah
blah fucking blah, some of us want to get on with life. Funny,

that. How we did, and life does, it carries on. For the lucky ones.
I can't rightly say whether we choose it, or it us, but I'm standing
here on the safe side of every near-sinking, the imagined memory of
blood on my tongue: I put our lips to her scored skin, stoned, and
the only sacred knowledge I'll ever know flooded in and through
and left me with that sound, sad laughter, and you. We open
the car doors and step out into the settling dust. The stars
above surge like the sea. Everything occurs within
and without me. We're drowning in the endless air. Share

one last smoke then, and this daydream: the son
you might have had is standing on the shore gazing
up into the northern sky. He's four now, going on
forty-five. He has her eyes, your physique, that troubled
sense of freedom. Time has softened your edges
like beachglass, waterstone, though there's still
the sharpness, molecular structure, beneath the surface.
Which god broke you? Does it matter? *It's all fun and games,*
she said, *till somebody gets hurt.* But we're not playing

anymore. This is the life you could have lived, the one
I've created and carried through the years, a sort of penance
its furthering, maintenance. Your old boat, *Five Fishes,*
is anchored just beyond the low waterline. What if
I kiss the scar on your wife's forehead, the crown
of your son's head, your wind-creased cheek? Farewell.
I'm wading out into the bay, walking, then swimming
towards the old wood hull. The deck is dark, work-
grimed, weathered, obsolete. I've been fishing these waters

for twenty years with your ghost inside me,
wind-wave, your wake-swell. I fire the main,
raise the hook, and motor out into the wide strait.
When I'm beyond the throw of town lights, I strip
the diesel line from the oil stove, strike a match
and drop it to the galley floor. From the water
I watch it burn. Does it seem like a bright star
from your distant shore? I'm moving further
from where you stand, your wife and son, hand

in hand. He has your reckless exuberance bursting
from within, curiosity like an affliction. I can hear
his little voice carry across the sea I'm swimming
inside myself. *So, does the universe just go on and on
forever then, or what?* he asks, swinging his gaze
from the burning boat to the flickering stars. You
pause for a moment, don't you, to consider the
wonder and sadness of the question. *Yes, son, forever,
it goes on and on,* you answer. *Isn't that something?*

## Acknowledgements

The epigraph is from Tomas Tranströmer's poem "The House of Headache," translated by John Matthias and Lars-Hakan Svensson.

This book was written with the financial assistance of the Canada Council for the Arts and the British Columbia Arts Council.

Thanks first and foremost to Jan Zwicky, for your kind words, for believing in this book, and for helping me to keep focused on and trust its centre.

To Steven Heighton, for your kind words and thoughtful insights.

To John Pass and Theresa Kishkan, for seven years of abiding "Well, I'm working on this long poem..." conversations.

To Silas White and everyone at Nightwood Editions.

To Amy Bespflug, always.

This book is for Chrys, Clint, Curtis and Quincy Sample.

## About the Author

Joe Denham is the author of the poetry collections *Flux* (Nightwood, 2003) and *Windstorm* (Nightwood, 2009), and the novel *The Year of Broken Glass* (Nightwood, 2011). His work has appeared in numerous magazines and anthologies including *Breathing Fire 2: Canada's New Poets* (Nightwood, 2004) *Open Field: 30 Contemporary Canadian Poets* (Persea, 2005) and *The New Canon: An Anthology of Canadian Poetry* (Signal, 2005). He lives with his wife and two children in Halfmoon Bay, BC.